MW00896680

☆ Thank you for your

We hope this book will help your kids to learn basic mathematical skills such as number recognition, number tracing, counting, addition, and subtraction.

Contact us: www.rvappstudios.com

First paperback edition **February 2023**

Designed by: RV AppStudios Team

ISBN: 9798375145662

About us

· · · · ● · · ·

We create amazing children educational books for babies, toddlers, and little kids. Lucas & Friends by RV AppStudios is one of largest children's mobile app developers in the world. Over 150 million kids will play with our apps this year, and that's for free and with no ads.

PRESCHOOL MATH

Activity Book

2 3

1

This book belongs to:

_____

Created by

3+2

5-2

Say and trace the number 0

1 2

0 0 0 0

0 0 0 0

zero zero zero

zero zero zero

Color all '0's

Circle the number 0

Say and trace the number I

Circle the number 1

Write '1' on each balloon

Say and trace the number 2

Color 2 fish and 2 jellyfish

Color all the number 2

Say and trace the number 3

3   3   3   3

3   3   3   3

three three

three three

Count and color

Draw 3  apples on each tree

Say and trace the number 4

Count and match

1

3

4

2

Color any 4 birds

Say and trace the number 5

Count and color balloons

Color 5 vegetables

Say and trace the number 6

6 6 6 6

6 6 6 6

six   six   six

six   six   six

Color eggs that have number 6

Count and write the number

Say and trace the number 7

Color the object that has 7

Count and match

Say and trace the number 8

Count and write the numbers

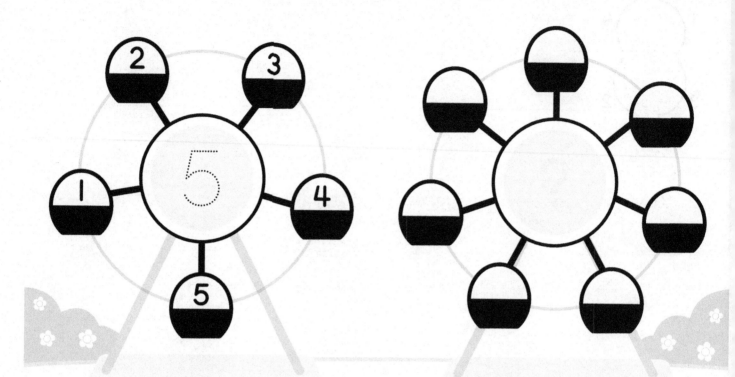

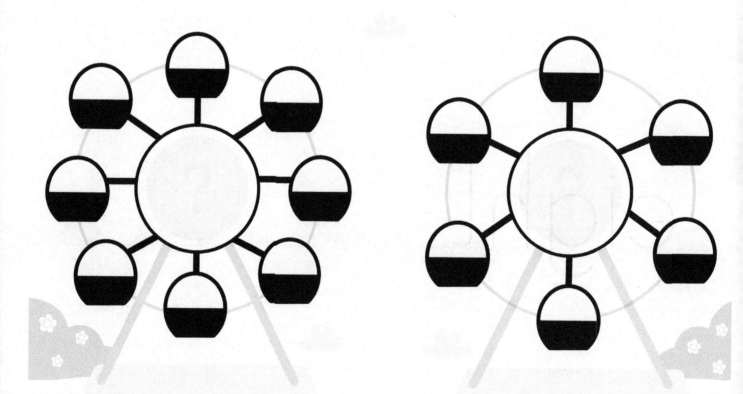

Fill the color by numbers

1 - YELLOW   2 - GREEN   3 - BLUE   4 - ORANGE

5 - PURPLE   6 - PINK   7 - RED   8 - BROWN

Say and trace the number 9

q q q q

q q q q

nine nine nine nine

nine nine nine

Find the number 9 and color

Count and circle the correct numbers

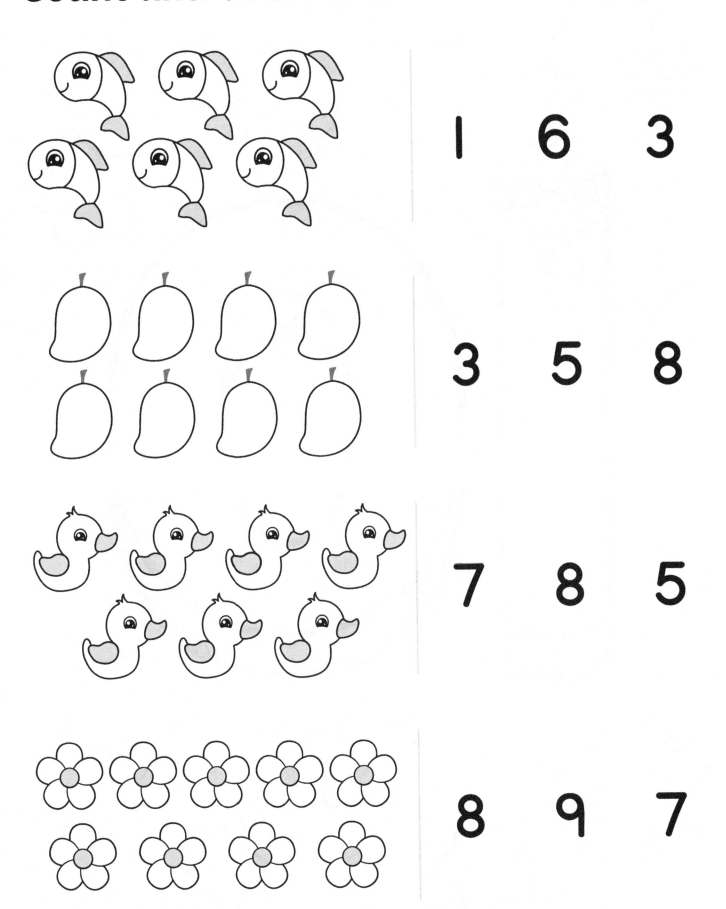

1   6   3

3   5   8

7   8   5

8   9   7

Say and trace the number 10

10 10 10 10 10

10 10 10 10

ten   ten   ten

ten   ten   ten

Count eggs and color the hen

Count and circle the correct numbers

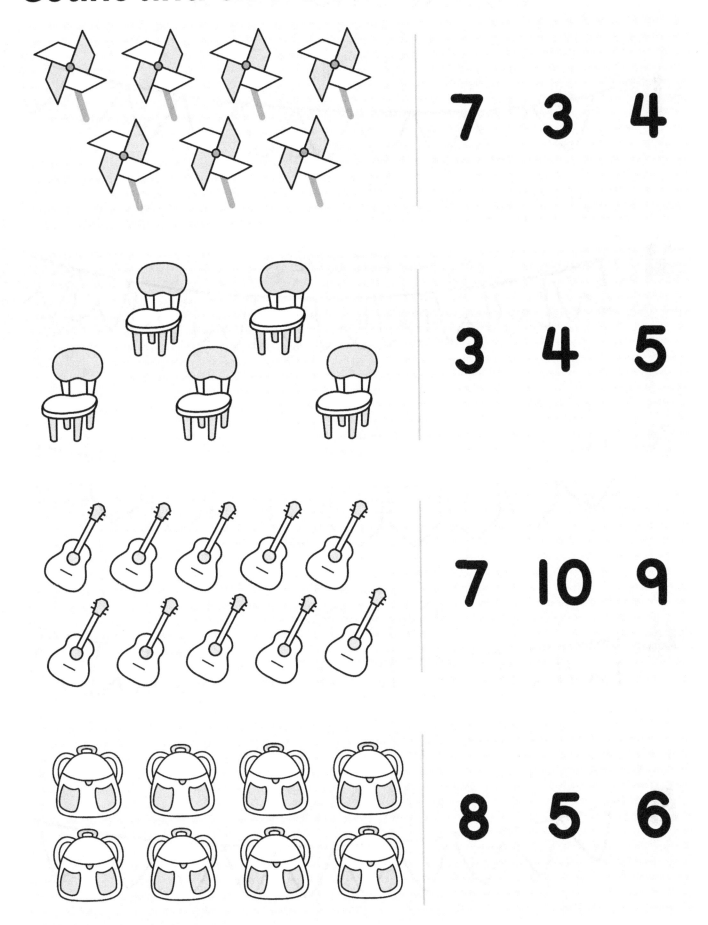

7   3   4

3   4   5

7   10   9

8   5   6

Count and color

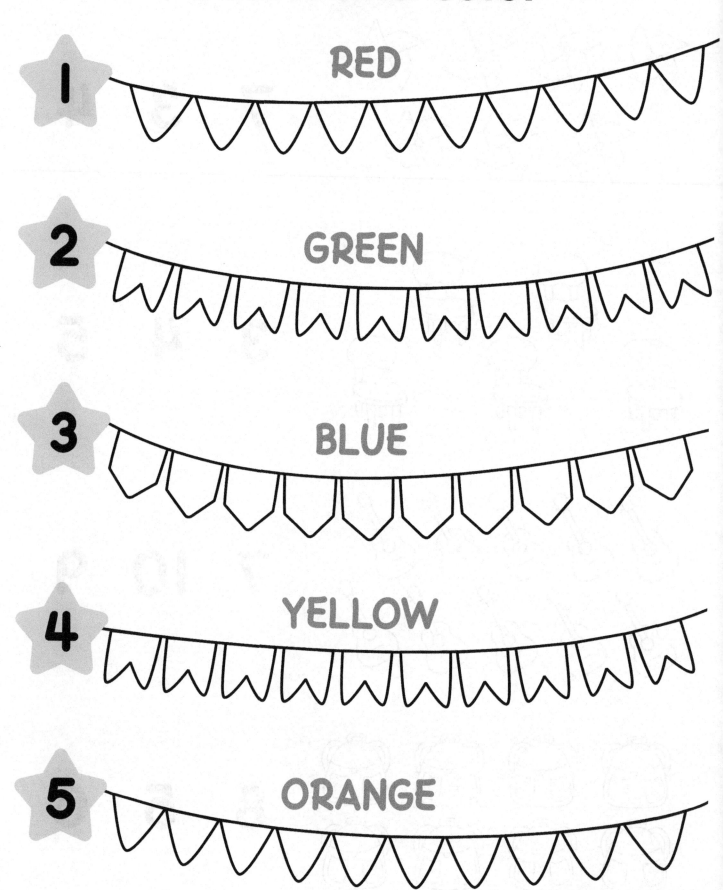

1 RED

2 GREEN

3 BLUE

4 YELLOW

5 ORANGE

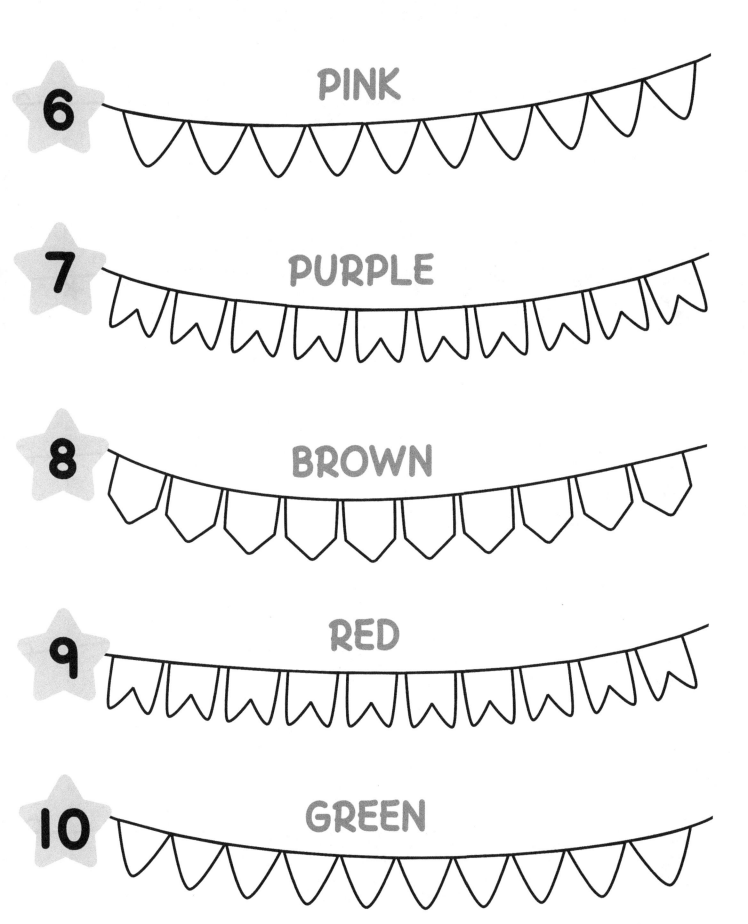

6 PINK

7 PURPLE

8 BROWN

9 RED

10 GREEN

Fingerprint coloring

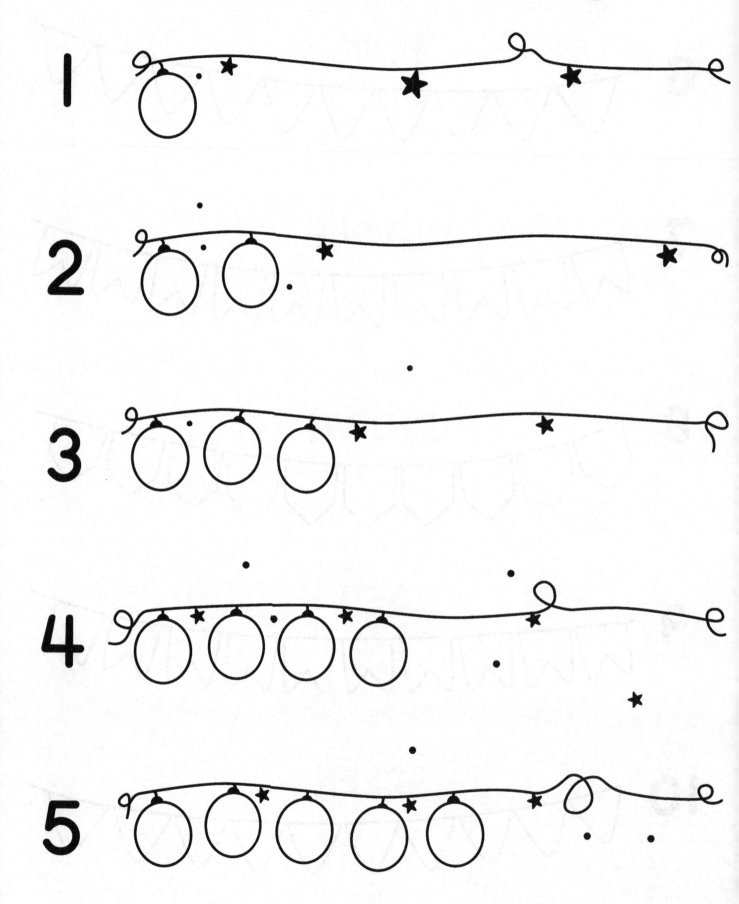

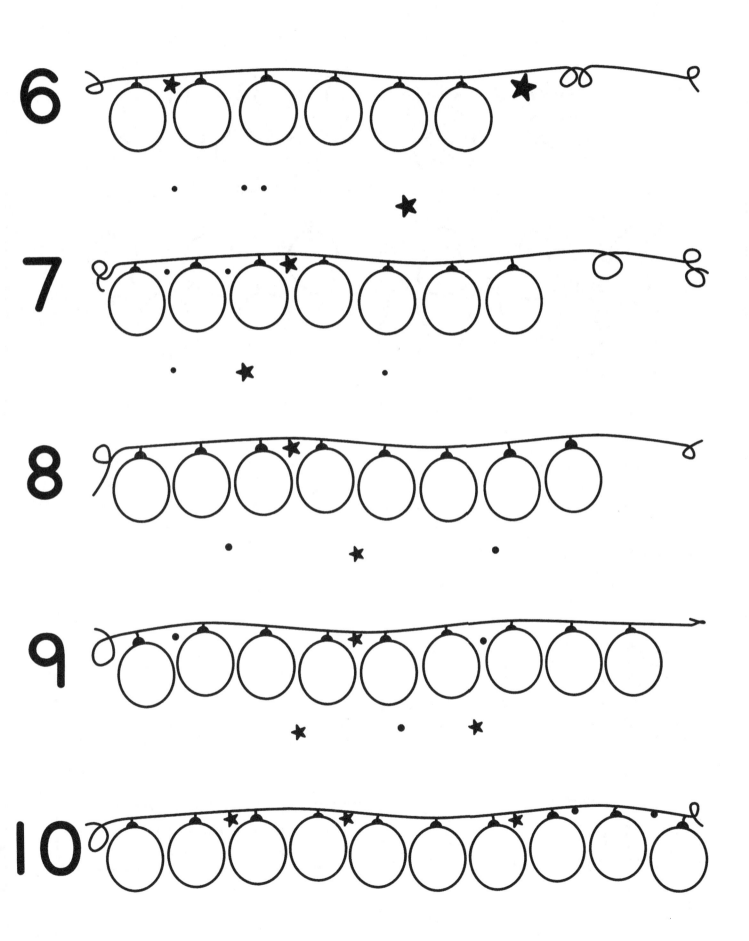

Count and write the number

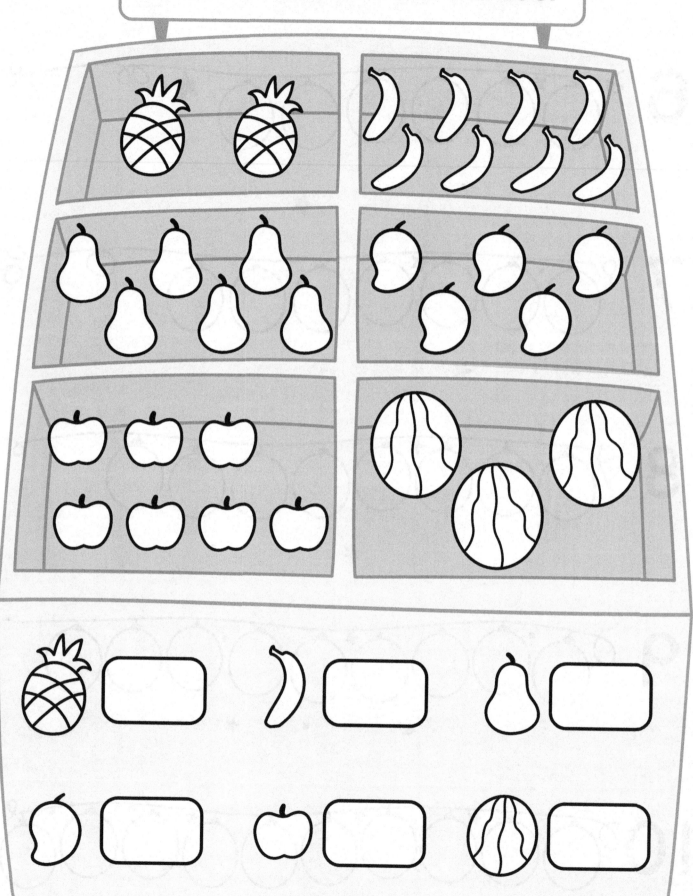

Connect the numbers

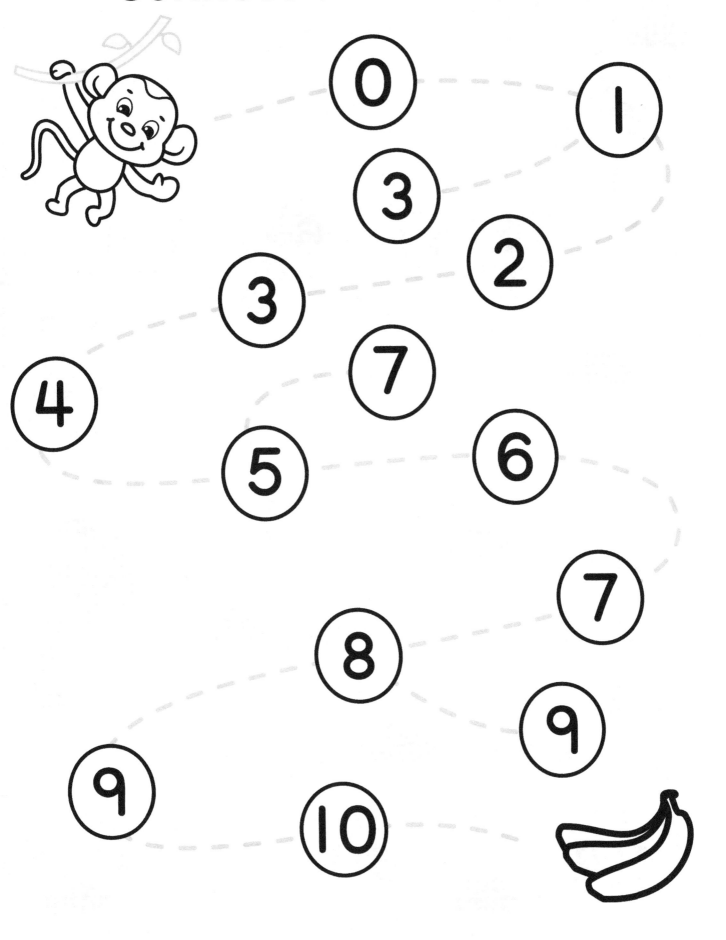

Fill in the missing numbers

1 _ 3 4 _ 6 _ 8 9 _

1 _ 3 _ 5 6 7 _ _ 10

1 2 _ _ 5 _ 7 _ 9 _

Number maze 1 – 10

Connect the dots and color

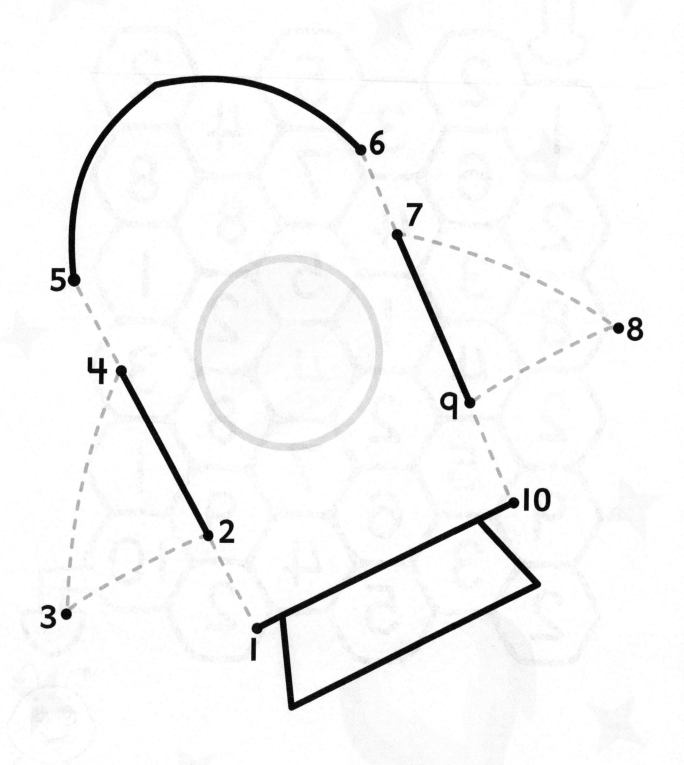

Draw and count

3 Ice creams

4 Hats

6 Eggs

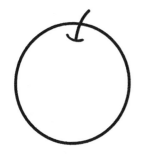

3 Oranges

5 Stars

Count and match

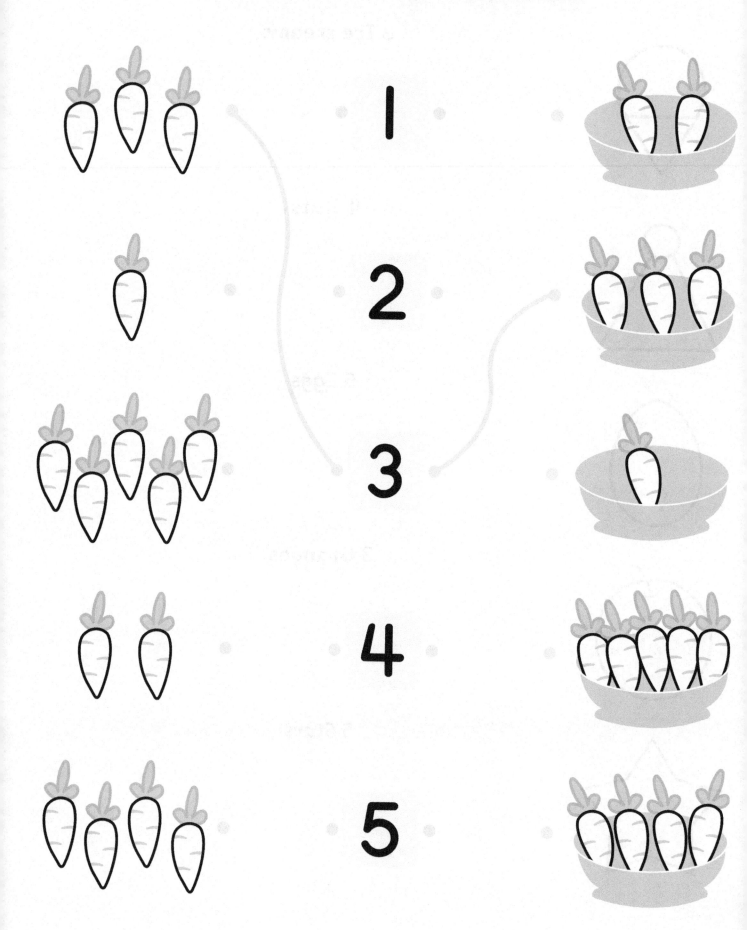

Count and match

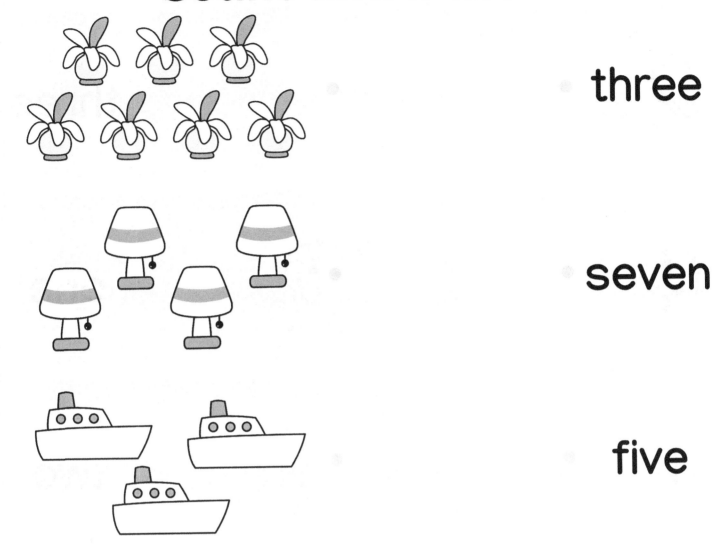

three

seven

five

four

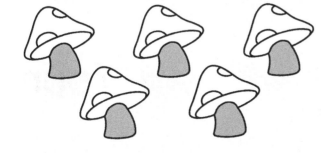

six

Count and match

2

three

4

one

1

two

5

five

3

four

Count and match

7   seven

8   six

6   ten

10   eight

9   nine

Circle the correct numbers

ONE

1 9 5

FOUR

4 5 7

SIX

10 6 1

TWO

6 4 2

THREE

3 7 2

EIGHT

4 8 2

TEN

9 5 10

FIVE

5 2 10

SEVEN

7 1 6

NINE

7 8 9

Fill in the missing letters

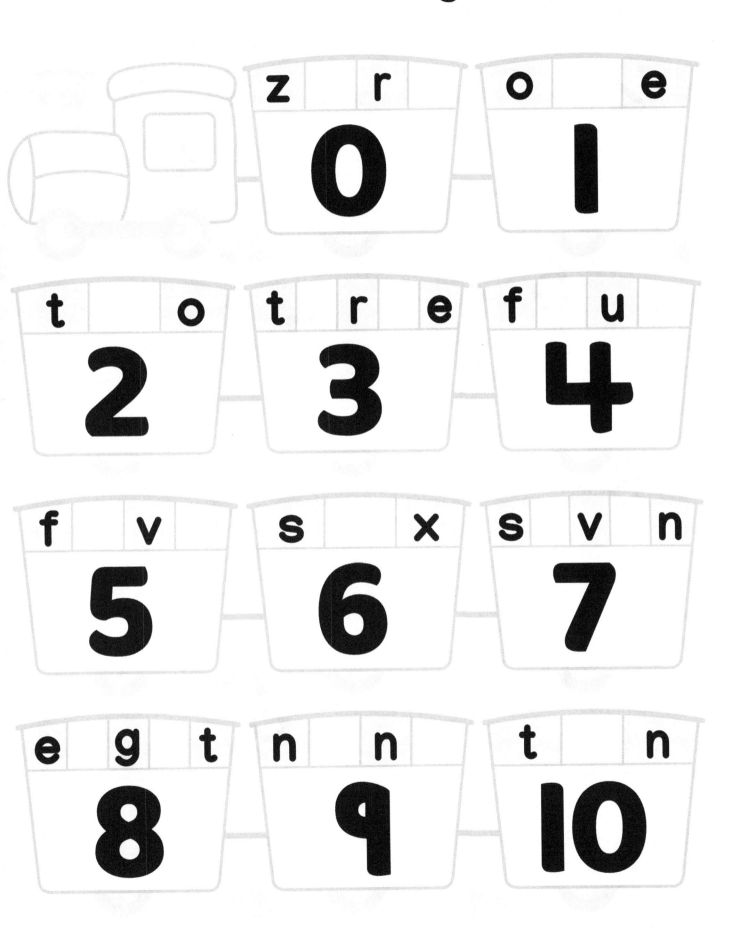

Write the number that comes after

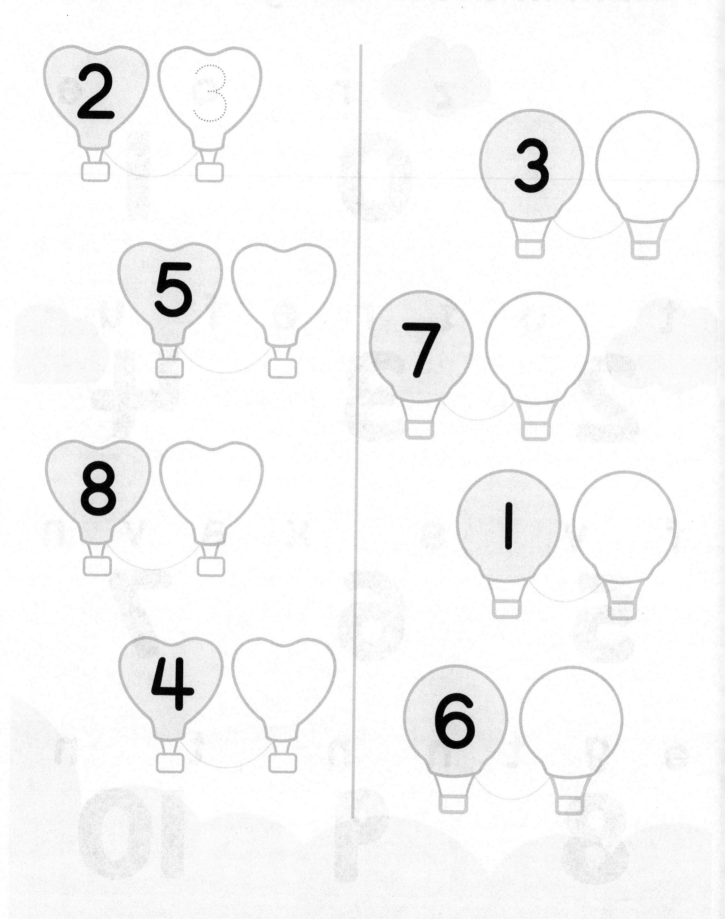

Write the number that comes before

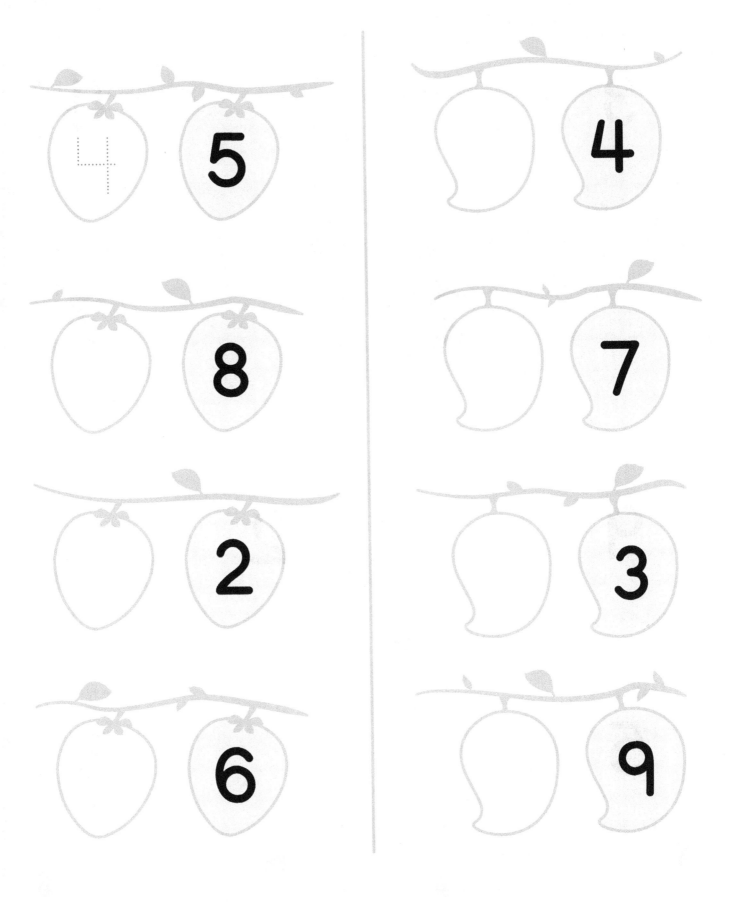

Fill in the number before and after

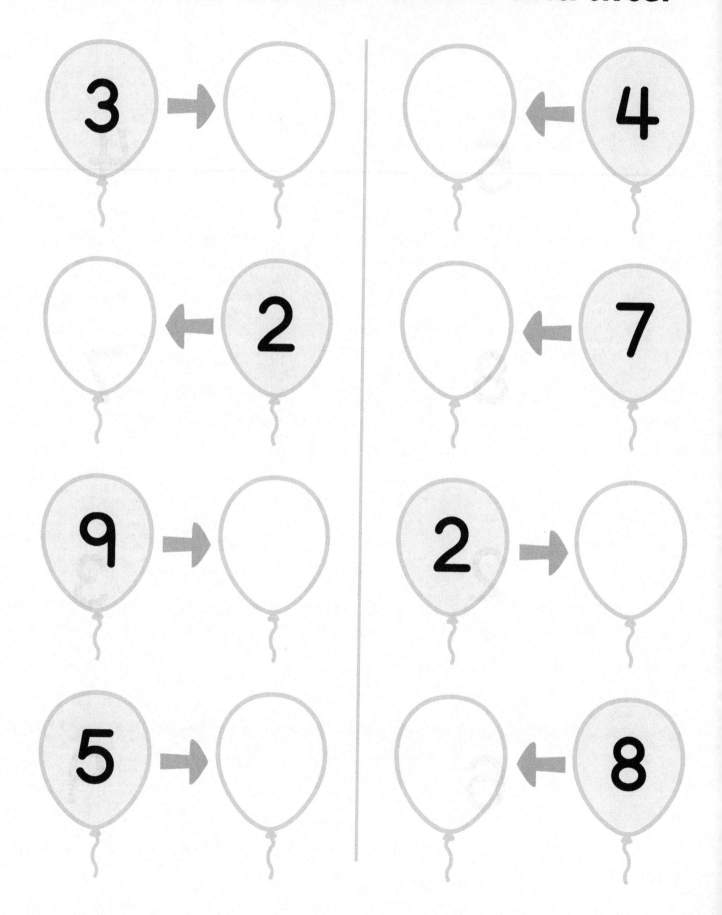

Write the number that comes in between

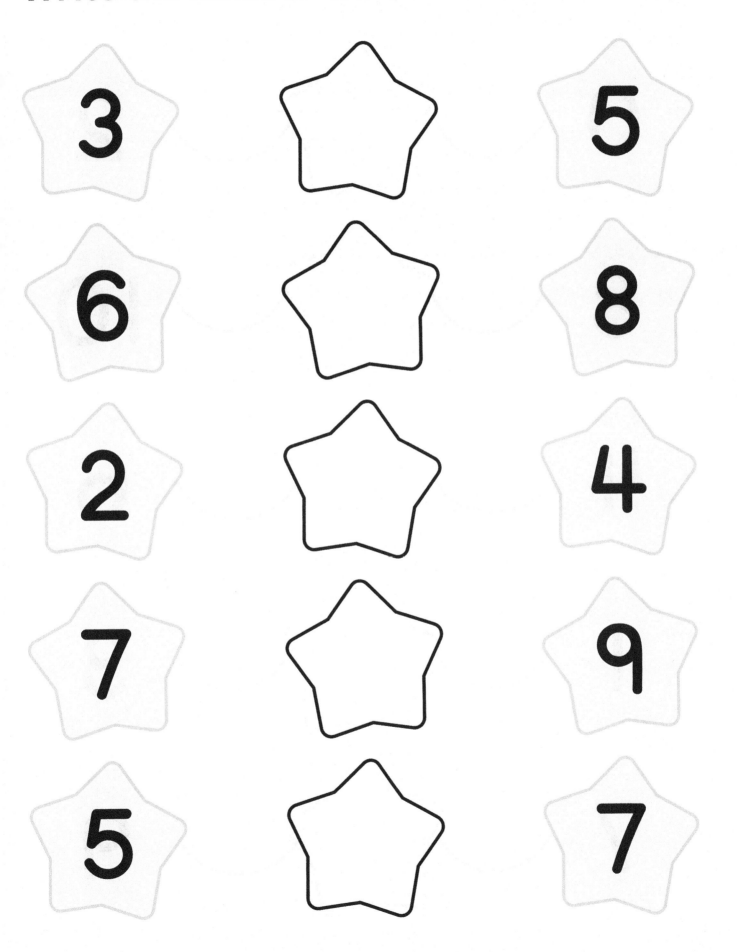

Write the number that comes in between

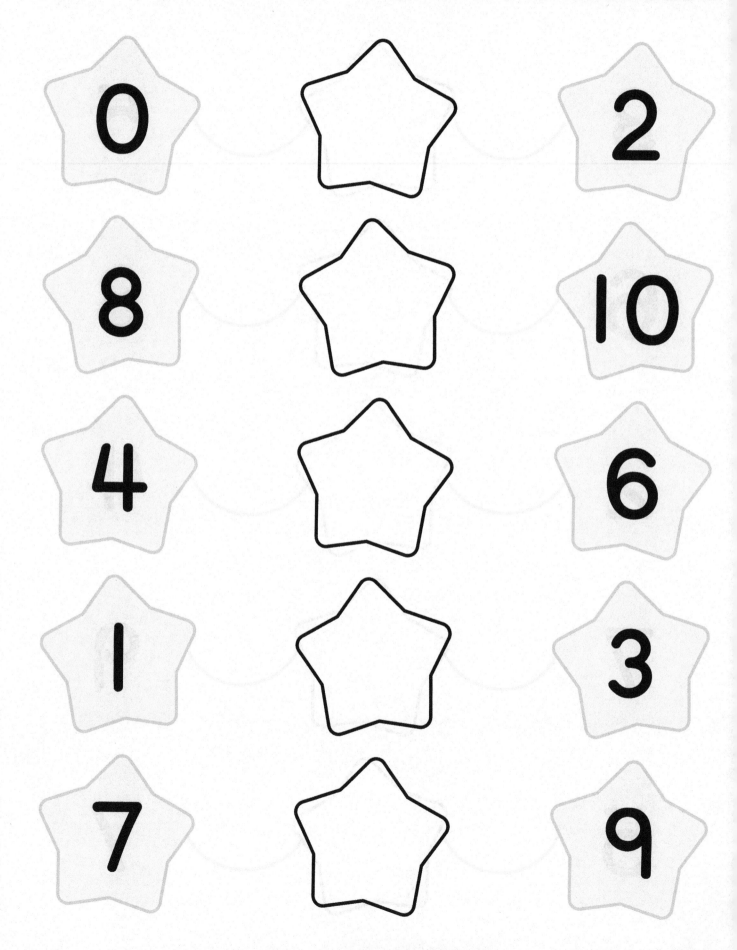

Which group has more?

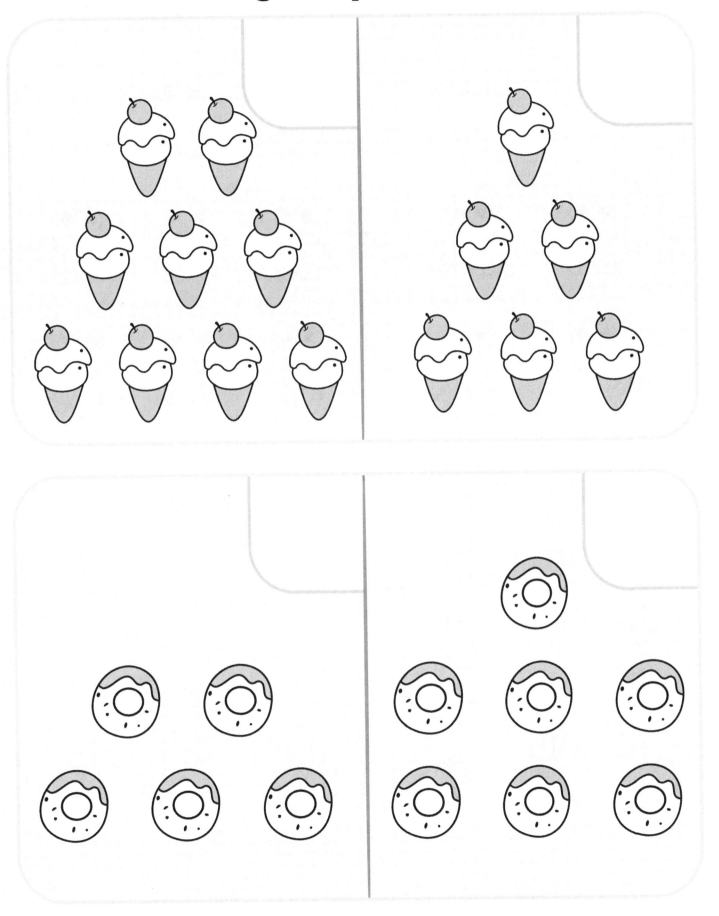

Which group has less?

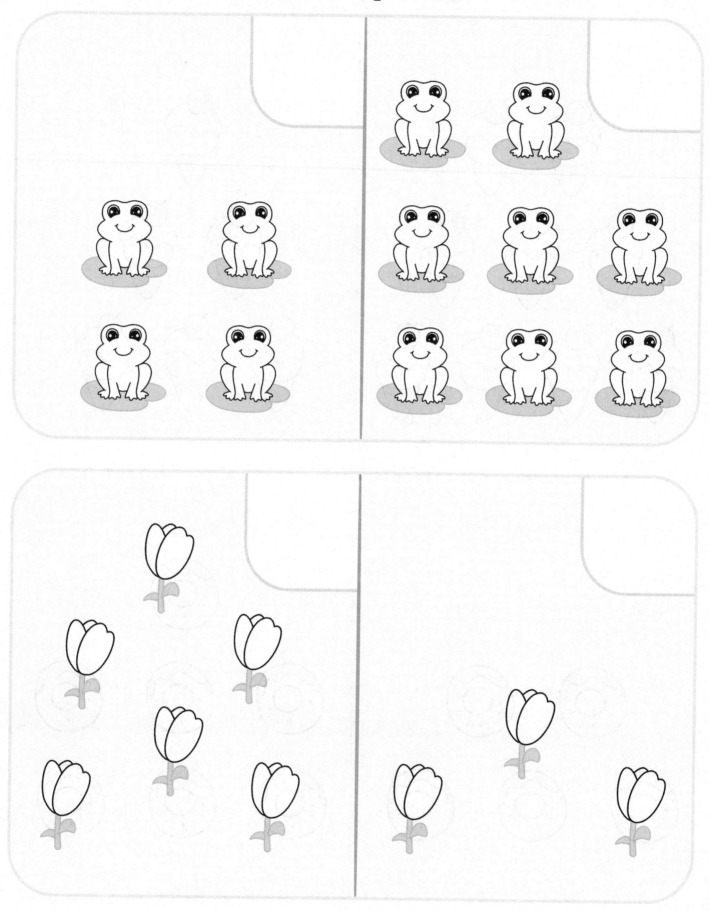

Circle the smaller numbers

(3)	5	8	2
2	1	9	7
8	9	6	9
5	4	8	5
3	9	2	3
6	5	10	9

Circle the bigger numbers

(2)   1   4   9

4   2   3   4

6   7   8   7

3   1   6   5

5   8   2   9

6   4   5   3

Skip counting by 2

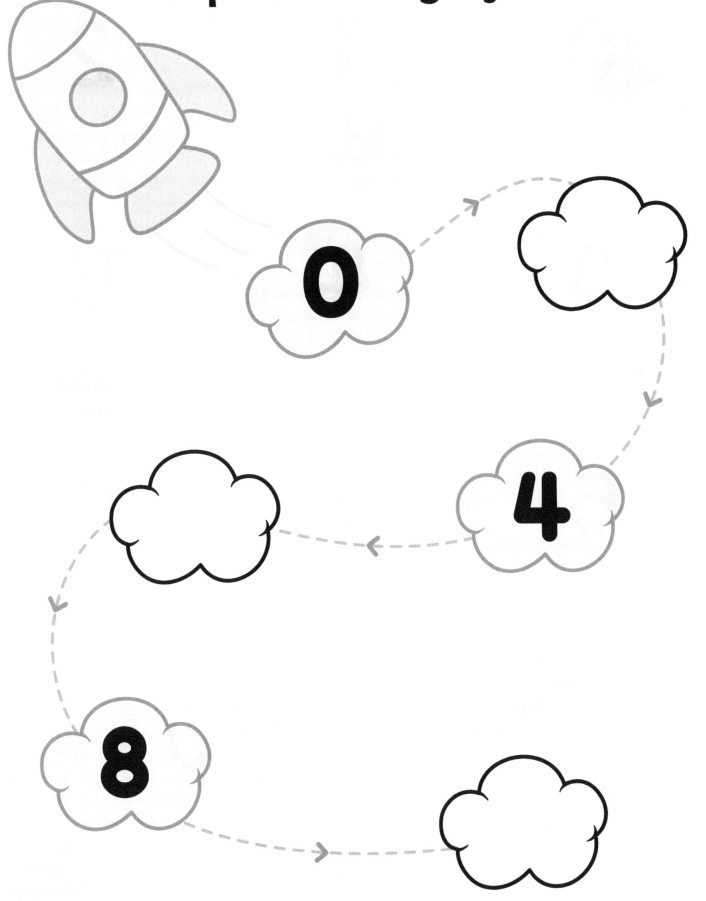

Trace and write the words

0   1   2

zero   one   two

3   4   5

three   four   five

6   7   8

six   seven   eight

9   10

nine   ten

✂

CERTIFICATE

OF EXCELLENCE IN COUNTING NUMBERS

This certificate is presented to

Trace the numbers

Addition

Count and add

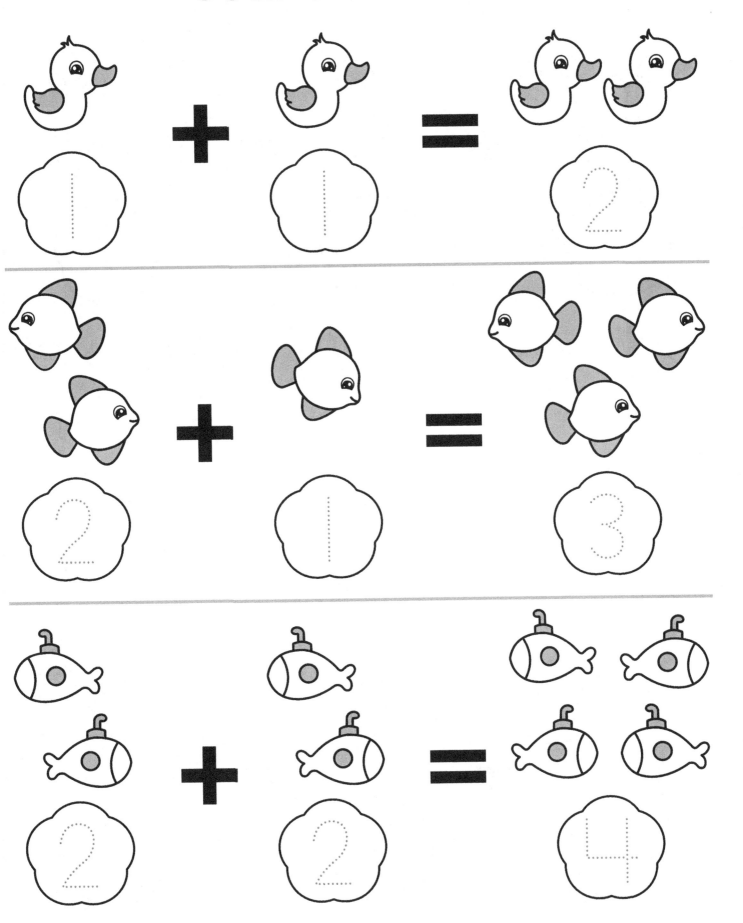

Count and add

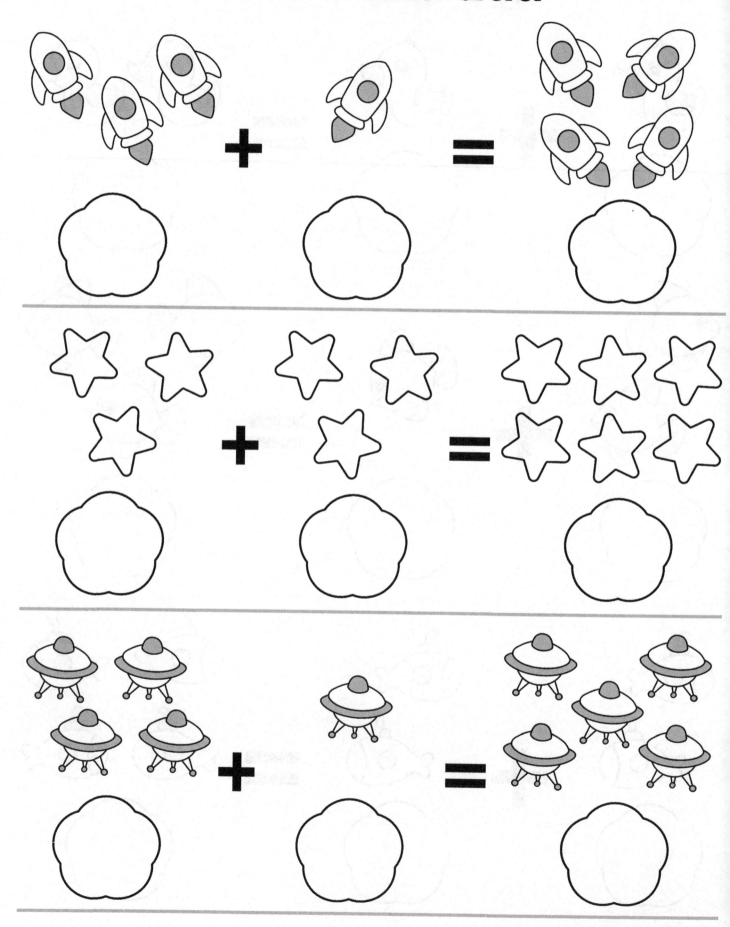

Count and add

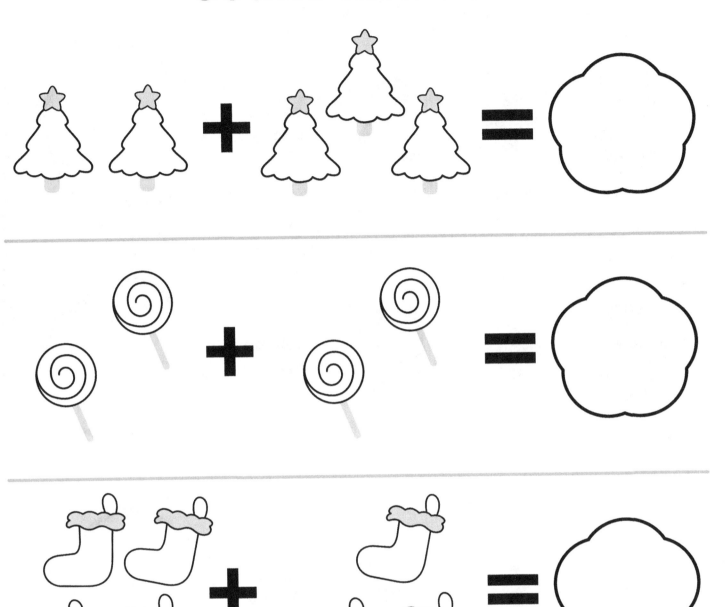

Fun addition

5 + 3 =

6 + 4 =

7 + 2 =

6 + 1 =

Fun addition

$$2 + 5 = $$

$$4 + 4 = $$

$$9 + 1 = $$

$$2 + 7 = $$

Add and match

Fun maze addition

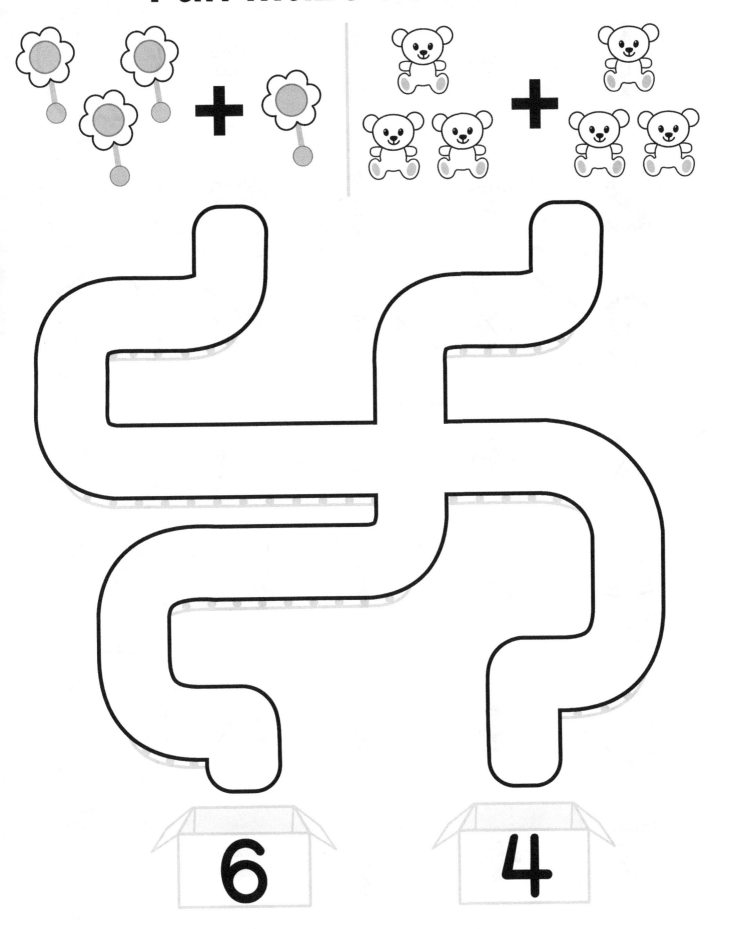

Addition by 1

1 + 1 = ⬡

2 + 1 = ⬡

3 + 1 = ⬡

4 + 1 = ⬡

5 + 1 = ⬡

6 + 1 = ⬡

7 + 1 = ⬡

Add, count, and match

3+4

4+1

2+1

2+2

3+1

3+3

4+2

6+1

2+3

1+2

Fill the color by answer

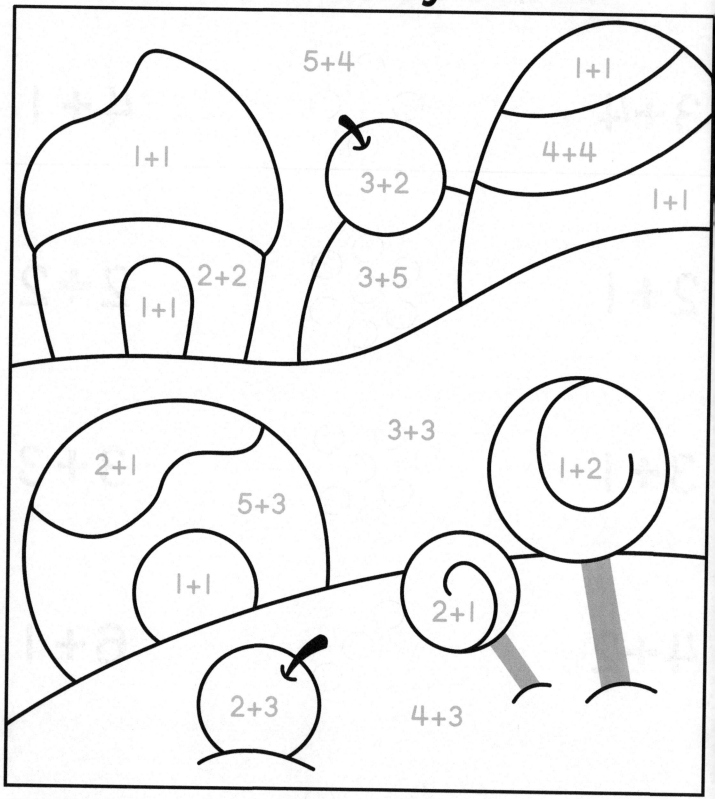

2 - YELLOW   **3 - PURPLE**   **4 - ORANGE**   **5 - RED**

6 - GREEN   **7 - BROWN**   **8 - PINK**   **9 - BLUE**

Fun addition

2 + 1 =

1 + 1 =

4 + 2 =

2 + 6 =

4 + 3 =

5 + 2 =

8 + 1 =

6 + 3 =

4 + 4 =

7 + 3 =

7 + 2 =

5 + 4 =

Make Lucas look cute by coloring it

Subtraction

Count and subtract

  $2 - 1 =$ 1

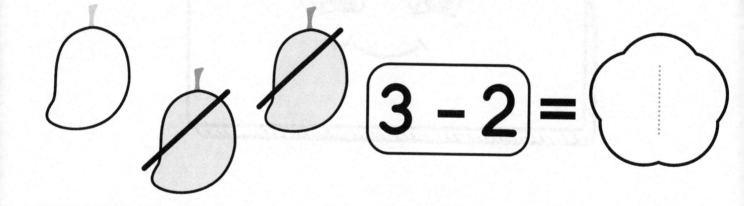 $3 - 2 =$ 1

 $4 - 2 =$ 2

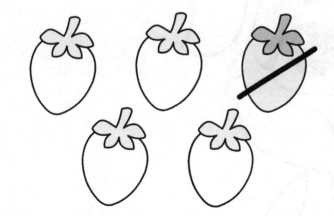 $5 - 1 =$ 4

Count and subtract

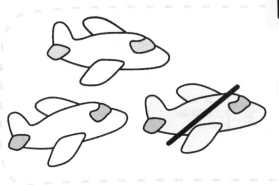 3 − 1 = 2

 4 − 1 =

 5 − 3 =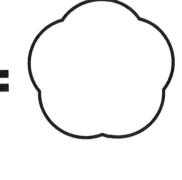

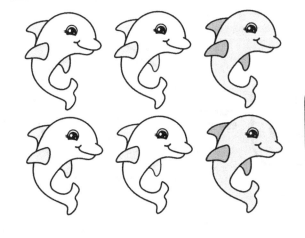 6 − 2 =

Count and subtract

$$4 - 3 = 1$$

$$6 - 3 =$$

$$5 - 2 =$$

$$7 - 3 =$$

Fun subtraction

5 - 3 =

5 - 1 =

7 - 2 =

8 - 5 =

Fun subtraction

8 - 2 =

6 - 4 =

9 - 1 =

7 - 5 =

Subtract and match

Subtract and match

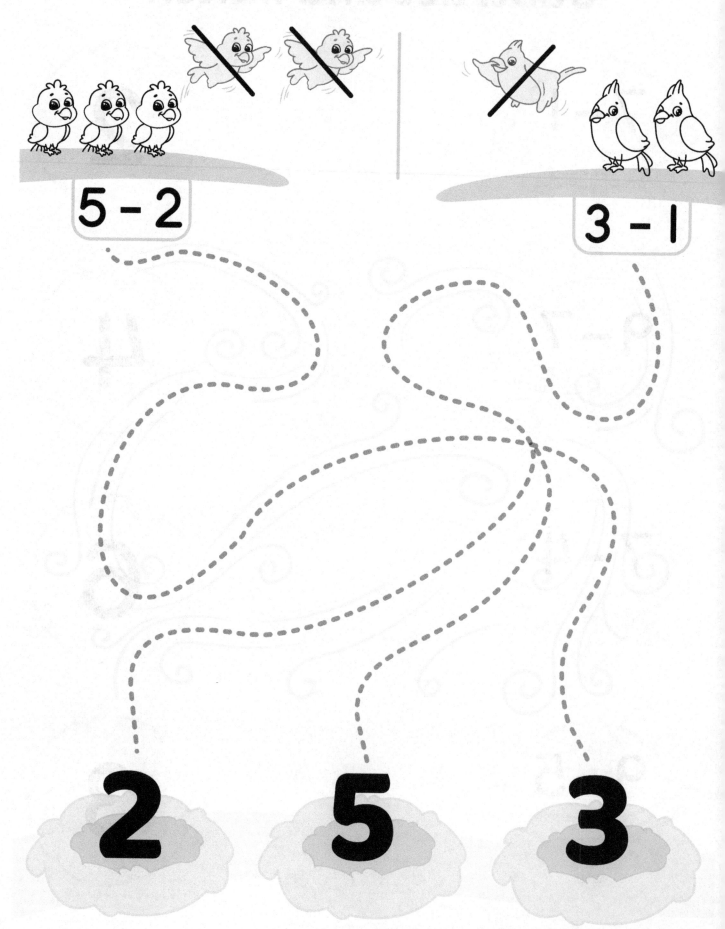

Subtraction by 1

2 − 1 =

3 − 1 =

4 − 1 =

5 − 1 =

6 − 1 =

7 − 1 =

8 − 1 =

Subtract, count, and match

3 − 1

5 − 2

6 − 1

9 − 3

9 − 2

8 − 1

7 − 2

4 − 2

10 − 4

6 − 3

Fun subtraction

4 – 1 =

5 – 3 =

5 – 4 =

8 – 5 =

7 – 4 =

8 – 2 =

7 – 2 =

9 – 3 =

10 – 9 =

8 – 6 =

9 – 1 =

10 – 3 =

Fill the color by answer

7−3   3−1   6−2   4−2

6−4   5−1   5−3

6−3   8−4

5−2

8−2   9−3

10−1

9−4   9−1   8−3

10−1   9−2

2 - YELLOW   **3 - GREY**   **4 - RED**   **5 - GREEN**

6 - PINK   **7 - BLUE**   **8 - BROWN**   **9 - ORANGE**

Addition and subtraction

1 + 1 =

2 + 3 =

2 - 1 =

3 + 6 =

6 - 3 =

7 - 6 =

8 + 1 =

7 - 2 =

8 + 2 =

9 + 1 =

10 - 7 =

10 - 4 =

Addition and subtraction

2 + 6 = ◯   1 + 6 = ◯

3 - 1 = ◯   3 - 3 = ◯

4 + 4 = ◯   5 + 2 = ◯

4 + 5 = ◯   5 + 5 = ◯

9 - 3 = ◯   7 - 3 = ◯

2 + 2 = ◯   10 - 5 = ◯

Fill the color by answer

2 - YELLOW   **3 - PURPLE**   **4 - RED**   **5 - GREEN**

6 - PINK   **7 - BLUE**   **8 - BROWN**   **9 - ORANGE**

Make Ruby look pretty by coloring it

CERTIFICATE

OF ACHIEVEMENT

This certificate is presented to

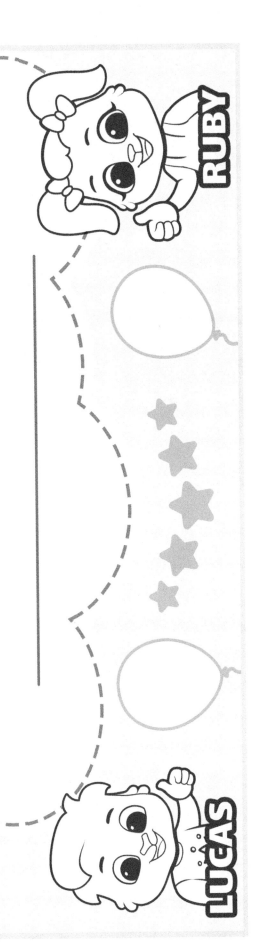

RUBY

LUCAS

Cut from perforated lines

Made in the USA
Columbia, SC
16 November 2024

46703956R00063